Snowy Day Bird Buffet

by Mary Helen Grasso

Illustratred by Brianne Seay

Published by: Awaken the Wonder (imprint)
ISBN: 978-1-7347830-0-1
Printed in the United States of America
The illustrations for this book were created in Adobe Illustrator by Brianne Seay.

This book is dedicated to the memory of my parents, Helen and Bob Seay, who instilled in me a love of birds and nature, and to my three grandchildren, James, Ellie, and Genevieve, who inspire me to continue writing and sharing my appreciation for all that is wondrous in our world.

Special thanks to my son, Eliot Grasso, for his encouragement, coaching, and unfailing support.

"You are not too small. No one is ever too small to offer help."

-Emlyn Chand from *Honey the Hero*

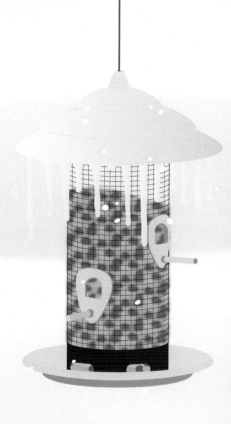

When Old Man Winter brings the snow
our backyard birds are hungry, so...

I put out seeds, all kinds, and suet.
If I don't help them, who will do it?

ONE lone grackle

eating bits of corn,
glad to have some breakfast
on this cold and icy morn.

TWO bold Jenny wrens

secretly my favorites,
perch and check around the deck,
then help themselves to tidbits.

THREE sleek nuthatches

climbing down the tree,
heard there was a bird buffet
and all the food was free.

FOUR brilliant cardinals

pecking through the seed,
looking for the black ones
'cause they're the kind they need.

FIVE downy woodpeckers

lining up to eat—
bricks of suet made of fat
are such a tasty treat.

SIX busy juncos

in coats of charcoal gray
scratch the snow to find
the seeds that almost got away.

SEVEN cheery chickadees

in stylish little caps
chirrup as they queue for lunch,
such charming chicks and chaps.

EIGHT bossy blue jays

chase the rest away
and take their share of what is there.
They always get their way!

NINE noisy
starlings
flapping as they squawk.
Nitter-natter, oh, such chatter!
So much raucous talk!

TEN stately mourning doves
line up on the wall,
picking up the bits of corn
and suet as they fall.

ELEVEN tufted titmice

with puffed out chests so rosy,
cock their heads from left to right,
alert and somewhat nosy.

TWELVE shiny cowbirds

jostle for a spot.
Greedy grabbers! Such bad manners!
What a boisterous lot!

My bird buffet is open for all my feathered friends.
I like to keep them going 'til the harsh, cold winter ends.

The big, the small, the drab, the bright, all colors may partake.
There's room for every hungry one with wings for heaven's sake!

Fun Fact No. 1:

Grackles eat a wide variety of foods including: seeds, berries, acorns, caterpillars, beetle grubs, grasshoppers, spiders, and even small rodents. Some have been known to dip hard bread crumbs in water to soften them before eating.

Fun Fact No. 2:

Wrens sometimes add spider egg sacs to their nests to combat mites that might threaten their young. Wrens have also been known to add a piece of snake skin to their nests.

Fun Fact No. 3:

Nuthatches like to eat insects and large nuts which they will wedge into furrows in tree bark before hammering with their beaks, to hatch them open. This is how they got their name.

Fun Fact No. 4:

The cardinal is the state bird of seven states: Illinois, Indiana, Kentucky, North Carolina, Ohio, Virginia, and West Virginia. They were named for the red clothing worn by cardinals in the Roman Catholic Church.

Fun Fact No. 5:

Downy woodpeckers are the smallest woodpeckers in North America. The male woodpeckers have a bright red patch on the back of their heads which the females do not have. They help trees by eating harmful insects and larvae.

Fun Fact No. 6:

Juncos are sometimes called snowbirds. They are gray and white birds that often appear at bird feeders in winter. They are one of the most abundant forest birds in North America.

Fun Fact No. 7:

Chickadees are small, black-capped birds that get their name from their cheery call: "chick-a-dee-dee-dee." A chickadee weighs less than four sheets of computer paper. Males and females look alike and usually mate for life.

Fun Fact No. 8:

Blue jays are loud and colorful birds that eat almost anything. They sometimes rob other birds' nests of their eggs and young. Blue jays like living near oak and beech trees, in wooded suburbs, and city parks.

Fun Fact No. 9:

Starlings travel in huge flocks and are considered pests by many. They have had a negative impact on other hole-nesting birds like bluebirds and red-headed wood-peckers because they compete with them for nesting sites.

Fun Fact No. 10:

Mourning doves are one of the most common birds in North America and one pair may raise as many as 5-6 broods a year in warmer areas. The wings of mourning doves make a whistling sound when they take off and land.

Fun Fact No. 11:

Tufted titmice are gray birds with large black eyes and crests on their heads. They have peach-colored patches under their wings. One of their calls sounds like "peter-peter-peter."

Fun Fact No. 12:

Cowbirds get their name from following herds of bison and cattle to eat insects flushed out of the grasses by the cows. They lay their eggs in other birds' nests, leaving their young to be raised by host parents.

sources

audubon.org

allaboutbirds.org

backyardchirper.com

birdsandblooms.com

birdsna.org

britannica.com

theodysseyonline.com

tranquiloutdoors (Facebook)

Lesleythebirdnerd (YouTube)

glossary

abundant: plentiful, in great numbers

boisterous: rough and noisy

breeding: producing babies

brilliant: bright, vivid

broods: groups of young produced at one time

buffet: a meal laid out for guests to serve themselves

furrows: narrow grooves

jostle: push and shove rudely against others

partake: share along with others

queue: a line where customers wait for their turn

raucous: harsh, rowdy, disorderly

stately: elegantly, in a dignified way

suet: waxy, hardened fat from certain animals

author

Mary Helen Grasso is a writer and poet for the child in all of us. She is an observer and student of nature who wants to share her appreciation of the outdoors with others. When she isn't photographing birds, insects, and flowers she is visiting her grandchildren in Oregon where she spends time writing and illustrating books with them.

illustrator

Brianne Seay is an illustrator and graphic designer from Baltimore, MD. She enjoys watching Disney movies and baking. When she's not working on her next big project you can find her water-coloring, hiking, or finding new bakeries and coffee shops.

"You have to believe in happiness, or happiness never comes. Ah, that's the reason a bird can sing — on his darkest day he believes in spring."

-Douglas Malloch